Harriet
Beecher
Stowe

JUNIOR ■ WORLD ■ BIOGRAPHIES

Harriet Beecher Stowe

CELIA BLAND

CHELSEA JUNIORS

a division of CHELSEA HOUSE PUBLISHERS

Chelsea House Publishers

EDITOR-IN-CHIEF   Richard S. Papale
EXECUTIVE MANAGING EDITOR   Karyn Gullen Browne
COPY CHIEF   Philip Koslow
PICTURE EDITOR   Adrian G. Allen
ART DIRECTOR   Nora Wertz
MANUFACTURING DIRECTOR   Gerald Levine
SYSTEMS MANAGER   Lindsey Ottman
PRODUCTION COORDINATOR   Marie Claire Cebrián-Ume

JUNIOR WORLD BIOGRAPHIES

SENIOR EDITOR   Kathy Kuhtz

Staff for HARRIET BEECHER STOWE

ASSOCIATE EDITOR   Martin Schwabacher
COPY EDITOR   David Carter
EDITORIAL ASSISTANT   Robert Kimball Green
SENIOR DESIGNER   Marjorie Zaum
PICTURE RESEARCHER   Sandy Jones, Susan Biederman
COVER ILLUSTRATION   Bill Donahey

First printing

3 5 7 9 8 6 4 2

Library of Congress Cataloging-in-Publication Data
Bland, Celia.
   Harriet Beecher Stowe / Celia Bland
      p. cm.—(Junior world biographies)
   Includes biographical references and index.
Summary: A biography of the nineteenth century author famous for the novel
"Uncle Tom's Cabin" which denounced slavery and intensified the disagreement
between the North and South.
ISBN 0-7910-1773-7
ISBN 0-7910-1968-3 (pbk.)
1. Stowe, Harriet Beecher, 1811–1896 —Biography—Juvenile literature. 2.
Authors, American—19th century—Biography—Juvenile literature. 3.
Abolitionists—United States—Biography—Juvenile literature. [1. Stowe, Harriet
Beecher, 1811–1896. 2. Authors, American.] I. Title. II. Series.
PS2956.B57   1993
813'.3—dc20   92-17051
                                                                  CIP
[B]   AC

Contents

1   "I Will Write Something"   7

2   "Hattie Is a Genius"   17

3   "Porkopolis"   29

4   Success   41

5   Peace and Controversy   57

    Further Reading   73

    Chronology   74

    Glossary   76

    Index   78

When Harriet Beecher Stowe wrote Uncle Tom's Cabin, *she could not have dreamed what a tremendous impact her book would have on the world.*

1

"I Will Write Something"

The weary mother settled into the hard church pew, and the service began. Although she was a devout Christian, her mind was not on the sermon. Harriet Beecher Stowe had a right to be distracted. She was responsible for six children, and though her husband was a respected professor of religion, he did not make enough money to support the large family. But Stowe's thoughts were not on her own troubles. Instead she was concerned with a much bigger problem: slavery.

In her mind, an image formed of an old black man being beaten to death by two slaves at the orders of their white master. She could almost hear the old man's prayers as he died. Stowe rushed home and wrote down the vision that had come to her in church. When she read the scene to her children, one cried, "Oh, mamma! Slavery is the most cruel thing in the world!"

Stowe showed her husband, Calvin Stowe, what she had written. He, too, wept and begged her to write the rest of the story. The scene would become the climax of *Uncle Tom's Cabin*, one of the most important books in American history.

The year was 1851, and a fierce debate over slavery was raging throughout the United States. The conflict threatened to tear the young nation apart. In Brunswick, Maine, where the Stowes lived, slavery was illegal. But in the South, the law still allowed white people to buy, sell, and even kill black people without punishment.

Harriet Stowe well knew the sufferings of blacks under slavery. For 18 years she had lived in

Cincinnati, Ohio, just across the Ohio River from the slave state of Kentucky. When her own maid was discovered to be an escaped slave, she had helped the girl flee to the North rather than return her to bondage.

When Stowe and her family moved back to her native New England in 1850, they did not leave the question of slavery behind. The issue had burst into northern politics with the passage of the Fugitive Slave Act in 1850. Until then, most northern whites had turned a blind eye to slavery. But the new law forced northern states to allow slave catchers to kidnap blacks and send them back to slavery in the South. The slave catchers did not even have to prove their victims *were* escaped slaves. "It seemed now," Stowe later wrote, "as if the system [slavery] once confined to the Southern States was rousing itself . . . to extend itself all over the North, and to overgrow the institutions of free society."

Stowe vowed to lend her voice to the fight for freedom. Her father and brothers were

After the passage of the Fugitive Slave Act in 1852, opponents of slavery posted signs such as this one to warn blacks that they could now be captured and returned to slavery.

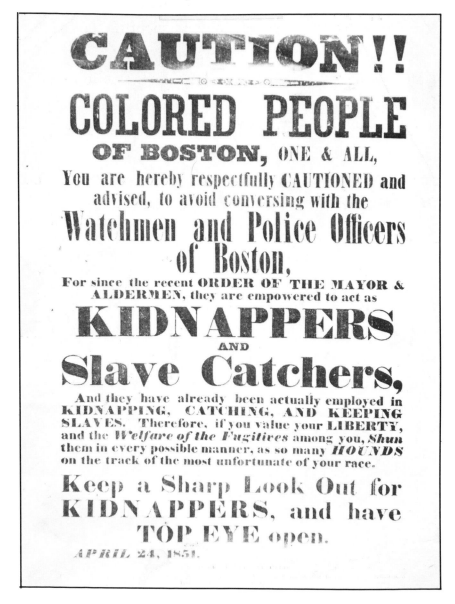

preachers whose powerful words made them national leaders. Harriet Stowe's passion and ability equaled that of the men in her family. But she was never given a chance to become a preacher because she was a woman. Instead, she had spent the last 14 years laboring as a wife and mother. The endless housework left her feeling at times like a "domestic slave."

Even during the hard years in Cincinnati, however, her talent with words could not be stifled. In spite of her duties as a mother and the frequent outbreaks of the dreaded cholera disease, which killed one of her children, Stowe found time to write. She sold many articles to newspapers and magazines to supplement the family income.

In the year of her move to Maine, time was especially scarce. She had her seventh child and started a school for girls with her sister Catharine Beecher, a leading educator. Even so, she began writing for an *abolitionist* (antislavery) journal, the *National Era*. A story she wrote called "The Freeman's Dream: A Parable," in which she argued against the Fugitive Slave Act, gave her a sense of the power her words could have in the fight against slavery.

Her determination increased when she received a letter from Isabella Beecher, her brother Edward's wife. "If I could use a pen as you can," Isabella wrote, "I would write something that will make this whole nation feel what an accursed thing slavery is." As she read the letter aloud to her family, Stowe rose from her chair, crushed the letter in her hand, and vowed, "I will write something. I will if I live."

It took great courage to write a book about slavery. As she later wrote, "this subject was a dangerous one to investigate." The abolition of slavery was not a popular cause even in New England. In Cincinnati, angry mobs had destroyed the printing press of an abolitionist paper and attacked the publisher. A friend of Stowe's brother Edward had been killed by such a mob. Stowe would be risking the safety of her family by joining what she called the "small, despised [hated], un-

In this portrait of the distinguished Beecher family, Harriet's father, Lyman Beecher, sits surrounded by his children. In back are five of his seven sons, all preachers. In front are his daughters—two reformers, a homemaker, and an author.

fashionable band" of outspoken abolitionists. Furthermore, she knew she would face criticism for speaking out on political issues at a time when this was considered impolite for women.

Fortunately, her family supported her plan. Her famous brother, Henry Ward Beecher, often gave fiery abolitionist sermons at his church in Brooklyn, New York. In January 1851, after giving a speech in Boston, he fought his way through a howling blizzard to visit his sister. The two stayed up all night talking about their plans to fight slavery. She told him, "I have begun a story, trying to set forth sufferings and wrongs of the slaves." "Do, it, Hattie," her brother urged. "Finish it."

It was in the following month that the powerful scene for the end of her book came to her in church. From then on, the words poured out of her. She felt as if it were not she who was writing *Uncle Tom's Cabin* but God. Stowe offered the story to the editor of the *National Era*, who agreed to publish it in weekly installments.

The response was incredible. For 40 weeks, the paper sold out every issue. On March 20, 1852, the tale was published in book form. In two days, all 5,000 copies had been sold. Sales reached 50,000 in a few months, and by the end of the year, 300,000 copies had been sold in America. International sales reached 1.5 million. One British journal declared that "the sale of *Uncle Tom's Cabin* is the most marvelous literary phenomenon that the world has ever witnessed."

In the North, Stowe's novel raised an outcry against slavery. In the South, it provoked anger and hatred. Slavery could no longer be ignored. *Uncle Tom's Cabin* forced the nation to address an issue that in the end would be resolved only by the Civil War. When Abraham Lincoln met with Stowe in the White House in 1863, he greeted her by saying, "So this is the little lady that made this big war."

Harriet Beecher, the sixth of 11 children, grew up in a strict religious household. As a child, she immersed herself in her imagination through reading.

2

"Hattie Is a Genius"

Harriet Beecher was born on June 14, 1811, the sixth child of Lyman and Roxana Beecher. When Harriet was only five years old, her mother died of *tuberculosis*. Although Lyman remarried the following year, Harriet would always be much closer to her father than her stepmother.

The son of a blacksmith, Lyman Beecher was a man of tremendous energy. He amazed his neighbors by building a set of exercise rings and parallel bars in his yard and swinging about on them. In bad weather, he would grab a shovel and dig into a pile of sand he kept in the basement for that purpose. He loved to roughhouse and play with his children, and they adored him.

"I remember him more as a playmate than in any other character during my childhood," Harriet's sister Catharine wrote. "I remember once he swung me out of the garret window by the hands, to see if it would frighten me, which it did not in the least."

Despite his working-class background, Lyman Beecher's powerful personality helped him to become a leader in his community. "The Lord drove me, but I was ready," he claimed. At 16, he attended Yale College to become a Calvinist minister.

Calvinism was a strict brand of Christianity that demanded total submission to God. Beecher's thundering sermons threatened that people's "souls are sleeping on the brink of hell." Rather than describing a kind, forgiving God, as many Christians do, Beecher's style of Calvinism told of an angry God, waiting to punish people for their sins.

Lyman Beecher was a minister at a time when people obeyed their religious leaders not only in matters of religion but in their politics and their personal lives as well. Beecher wielded a great deal of power in his community. He also provided a powerful role model for his children.

Beecher dominated his household just as he did his community. Although Harriet's mother, Roxana, was from an important family—her uncle was a general in George Washington's army—Lyman expected her to submit to him completely. Roxana had been raised to believe that she was "an object of God's mercy and goodness," but in their courtship, Lyman convinced her that she was "an enemy of God." He convinced her that she must obey not only God but her husband.

Harriet Porter Beecher, Lyman's second wife, was also "a lady of great personal elegance," according to her stepdaughter, but not well suited "for the bringing up of children of great animal

At a time when people looked to ministers for guidance in all matters, not just religion, Harriet's iron-willed father was a powerful presence in his community.

force and vigor." She bore 4 more children, raising the household total to 11, but she too found being the wife of a poor minister hard. Harriet's sister Mary wrote, "Mama is not well, and don't laugh anymore."

Lyman Beecher, however, thrived on the energy of his children. He led them in great debates over religious philosophy around the dinner table. The seven boys all took part, and these arguments provided excellent training for their future careers as ministers. No doubt Harriet would have become a minister too if she had been a boy, but less was expected of girls. In fact, when Harriet was born her father remarked, "Wish it had been a boy."

Harriet's intelligence could not be denied, however. By the time she was eight, Harriet was busily making her way through her father's books. "Hattie is a genius," he wrote. "I would give a hundred dollars if she was a boy." He enrolled Harriet in Miss Sara Pierce's school, the most prestigious school for girls in Litchfield.

When Harriet was 12, the school held an exhibition in the town hall. The teacher read aloud an essay that interested Harriet's father so much that he asked who had written it. Harriet beamed with pride as her father learned that she was the author.

Lyman was proud of Harriet's abilities, but he did not think she was religious enough. "She is as odd as she is intelligent and studious," he wrote. He warned her that she "must break up the habit" of daydreaming "or be damned." But Harriet loved fantastic stories like *The Arabian Nights*, which she learned by heart. One summer she read *Ivanhoe*, Sir Walter Scott's tale of knights and chivalry, seven times. Most of all, she loved the romantic poetry of Lord Byron.

But her father's strict religion, with its constant warnings about hell and sin, took their toll on Harriet. "My whole life is one continued struggle. I do nothing right," she wrote her brother Edward. Fortunately for Harriet, her oldest sister, Catharine, was there to take her under her wing.

The Hartford Female Academy, founded by Harriet's sister Catharine. Harriet left home at age 12 to attend the school, where her talents blossomed; by age 16, she was a full-time teacher.

Catharine was 11 years older than Harriet and quite independent. She had a strong personality like her father and eventually became a national leader in the field of education for women. In 1823, at the age of 23, Catharine had already started her own school in Hartford, Connecticut.

Well knowing the struggles Harriet would face under their father's strict religious system, Catharine invited Harriet to enroll in her school. In 1824, at the age of 13, Harriet left home to travel the 30 miles to Hartford.

Over the next two years, Harriet studied writing, arithmetic, Italian, and French, and taught herself Latin from a textbook. In her spare time, she even began writing a verse drama in the style of her idol, Lord Byron.

In 1826, however, Lyman Beecher got a new job at a bigger church. He took Harriet out of Catharine's school and moved the family to Boston, Massachusetts. Harriet became deeply depressed. Henry Ward Beecher, the brother she was closest to, described her as "owling about." She tried to hide her unhappiness from her parents but wrote to Catharine, "I wish I could die young . . . rather than live, a trouble to everyone."

Catharine convinced their father to allow Harriet to return to school in Hartford. There Harriet threw herself into her studies, often working from nine in the morning till after dark. At the age of 16, she became a full-time teacher.

Harriet might have remained a teacher, one of the few jobs open to women at the time, had not Lyman Beecher's church caught fire and burned to the ground in 1830. The city's firefighters refused to put out the flames because they disliked Beecher for his crusade against alcohol.

Although Beecher did not know it, a liquor merchant had rented storage space in the church's basement. Hundreds of people watched in amazement as jugs of rum exploded in the heat of the

Harriet (left); her brother Henry Ward Beecher, who became the nation's leading religious reformer; and her sister Catharine Beecher (right), who, as an ambitious and successful woman, offered Harriet a powerful role model.

fire. Jokes about "Beecher's broken jugs" spread throughout the city. When Beecher tried to raise money to rebuild the church, he got little support.

Thousands of settlers were moving west at the time. Seeing a chance to shape the religious future of the country, Beecher decided to bring his message to the frontier. "If we gain the west all is safe," he said, "if we lose it, all is lost." He accepted a job as president of Lane Seminary in Cincinnati, Ohio. In 1832, 10 Beechers, including Harriet and Catharine, set out for the Queen City of the West.

In Cincinnati, Harriet met and married Calvin Stowe.
Calvin was a loving husband and a respected scholar
but had difficulty supporting his family financially.

3

"Porkopolis"

"I never saw a place so capable of being rendered a Paradise," wrote Catharine Beecher of Cincinnati. Harriet agreed—at first. Set on a group of hills along the north bank of the Ohio River, Cincinnatti had a population of 30,000 as well as many lovely homes and stately buildings.

But Cincinnati was also known as "Porkopolis" because of its foul-smelling slaughterhouses and meat-packing plants. Pigs roamed the garbage-strewn streets looking for food, and frequent cholera epidemics ravaged the town. Harriet summed up her opinion of the place when she saw

29

her four-year-old half brother playing with a hog. "Very disgusting," she wrote.

Even more disturbing for Harriet was the issue of slavery. In New England it had seemed a distant problem, but it was now a reality. Cincinnati was just across the Ohio River from the slave state of Kentucky. Cincinnati papers carried advertisements offering large rewards for the return of runaway slaves. She could see escaped slaves and hear their stories.

In June 1833, she got a glimpse of slavery firsthand when she and her friend Mary Dutton visited a Kentucky plantation. They stayed in an elegant house surrounded by smooth lawns. During the day, they watched slaves labor in the fields of corn, hemp, and tobacco. In the evenings, the plantation owner and his guests feasted on duck, chicken, turkey, and ham. Afterward, they sat in the parlor while slaves were ordered to sing and dance for their entertainment.

On one of these evenings, Beecher and Dutton met a young woman whose skin was only slightly darker than their own. She was the child of a black woman and a white man, but a slave nonetheless. Harriet's vivid memory of this woman later served as the basis for the character Eliza in *Uncle Tom's Cabin*.

In Cincinnati, most of Harriet's time was spent working at a new school Catharine had started, the Western Female Institute, where Harriet taught six days a week. She also wrote a geography textbook and many articles for local magazines and newspapers, the first appearing in June 1833.

Beecher was so busy that she found little time to socialize with anyone other than her family and Lane Seminary's faculty and students. One young man she met described her as "rather careless of dress & manner & absent minded," but also "feminine, kind, & with a quick apprehension [sense] of humor, which pleased us very much."

In August 1833 she made two very important friends: Professor Calvin Stowe, then in his early thirties and a teacher of religion at Lane

Seminary, and his wife, Eliza. Harriet and Eliza became best friends, and they often attended antislavery meetings at the seminary.

But tragedy struck the Stowe household in 1834. That summer, cholera swept through the city, and Eliza got sick and died. Harriet did her best to comfort the distraught Calvin Stowe while dealing with her own grief. As the two spent time together, they fell in love.

In many ways, Harriet and Calvin were a perfect match. She came from a family of preachers; he was a preacher. Both were from New England, and Calvin kept Harriet amused for hours telling her stories about his childhood in Massachusetts. Stowe was a respected Bible scholar and an inspiring speaker, and Harriet felt that these qualities made up for his inability to manage money, his love of food, and his constant illnesses. On January 6, 1836, they were married.

A few months after the wedding, Calvin Stowe left for an extended trip to Europe, where he was to purchase books for Lane Seminary's library. He was also asked by the Ohio legislature to examine the European schools. The legislators were so impressed by his report that they had 10,000 copies printed and distributed to every school in the state. Several other states reprinted his report as well.

Harriet had planned to go with him as far as New York, but she discovered that she was pregnant and was forced to cancel her plans. Wistfully, she wrote her husband as he prepared to sail: "My dear, I wish I were a man in your place; if I wouldn't have a grand time!" She moved in with her family and began writing articles for the *Western Monthly Magazine* and the Cincinnati *Journal and Western Luminary.*

On September 29, 1836, Stowe gave birth to twin girls. She named them Eliza Tyler Stowe, after Calvin's first wife, and Isabella Beecher Stowe. When Calvin returned from Europe in January 1837, he insisted that Isabella's name be changed to honor his new wife, so the baby became Harriet Beecher Stowe. The growing family

Some people called Cincinnati the Athens of the West, but others referred to the dirty frontier town as "Porkopolis" because of the many pigs that were butchered in its slaughterhouses.

moved into their own house and hired a young black woman as housekeeper.

Not long afterward, the Stowes found out that their maid, who claimed to be legally free, was in fact a runaway slave whose master was in Cincinnati searching for her. Calvin Stowe and Harriet's brother Henry Ward Beecher armed themselves with pistols and in the middle of the night smuggled the young woman out of the city by wagon. They took her to a farm that served as a stop on the *Underground Railroad*, the network of abolitionists who helped escaped slaves make their way north to freedom. The crisis left Harriet more upset about slavery than ever.

But her duties as a mother left her little time for political concerns. In January, she gave birth to a little boy she named Henry, and she became swamped by household chores. "I am a mere drudge with few ideas beyond babies and housekeeping," she wrote. As her depression returned, her sister Catharine commented, "I hope she is to have an interval of rest."

There would be no rest for the young wife and mother. In May 1840, she gave birth to another son, Frederick William. The difficult pregnancy and delivery left Harriet in bad health for a whole year. The family became even more poverty-stricken as Lane Seminary struggled and Calvin Stowe proved unable to support his growing family on his teacher's salary.

As debts mounted, Harriet again began to write. She published in many magazines. "If you see my name coming out everywhere," she wrote her friend Mary Dutton, "you can be sure of one thing—that I do it for the pay. I have determined not to be a mere domestic slave."

In August 1843, Harriet gave birth to her fifth child, Georgiana May, and her health again crumbled, leaving her bedridden for months. Again, she overcame her weakness and began to write. In 1843, her first book, *The Mayflower: Sketches of Scenes and Characters among the Descendants of the Pilgrims*, was published. Calvin Stowe was enthusiastic: "My dear, you must be a literary woman. It is so written in the book of fate."

Full of encouragement though he was, Calvin Stowe offered his wife little help in running the household. He was frequently away, and when at home, he often took to his bed, complaining loudly about various imaginary illnesses. In 1847, Calvin left for a visit to a Vermont spa. While he was gone disaster struck.

This anticholera poster warned against the danger of tainted food. In 1849, a cholera epidemic took the life of Stowe's infant son.

The summer of 1849 brought the worst cholera epidemic yet to Cincinnati. Thousands died, and as hearses rumbled through the streets, Harriet's new baby, Samuel Charles, went into convulsions. She wrote to Calvin, "We have been watching all day by the dying bed of little Charley, who is gradually sinking. There is no hope now of his surviving the night." The next day she wrote sadly, "Our dear little one is gone from us." But even in her grief she remembered the suffering of others. "I write as though there were no sorrow like my sorrow," she reflected, "yet there has been in this city . . . scarce a house without its dead."

When Calvin wrote that he had been offered a job at Bowdoin College in Maine, Harriet welcomed the news. It was with relief that Stowe and her family boarded the train back to New England. Little did she know that within two years of her arrival, her novel *Uncle Tom's Cabin* would make her one of the most famous people in America.

In 1862, Stowe met with President Abraham Lincoln in the White House and urged him to sign the Emancipation Proclamation, which would outlaw slavery in the South.

4
Success

When Harriet Beecher Stowe arrived in Maine in 1850, most northerners felt "not hostility to slavery, but indifference, and a reluctance to discuss it," according to George Templeton Strong, a prominent New Yorker. But the Fugitive Slave Act "made slavery visible in our communities," he wrote, following which *Uncle Tom's Cabin* set northerners "crying and sobbing over the sorrows" of the enslaved people.

Indeed, American slavery was one of the cruelest policies ever inflicted on one people by another. In all, 9 million Africans were kidnapped to be enslaved in America. In 1850, 3.2 million slaves toiled under the threat of the whip, working six days a week from dawn till dusk without pay. Rape of black women by their masters was common, as was the separation of children from their parents and wives from their husbands. One-third of all black families were torn apart by the sale of family members to different owners.

There had always been some opposition to slavery in America. Great black leaders like Frederick Douglass and Sojourner Truth wrote of their days in bondage and traveled widely to speak out against the horrors of slavery. In 1831, Nat Turner led an uprising in which slaves killed 57 whites before Turner was executed. An estimated 60,000 to 75,000 slaves escaped via the Underground Railroad.

Among whites, members of the Quaker religion, also known as the Society of Friends, were especially active in organizing antislavery groups. By 1838, there were about 1,350 abolitionist societies, with a total membership of

250,000. Many whites who opposed slavery, however, sim- ply wanted to send blacks back to Africa at some future date when they were no longer needed on plantations. Those calling for the immediate abolition of slavery were considered troublemakers and were sometimes attacked by angry mobs.

Stowe tried to show in *Uncle Tom's Cabin* that although many southern whites were good people, terrible suffering and abuse would continue as long as slavery existed. In the book, a kindhearted slave owner falls into debt and is forced to sell a boy away from his mother. Rather than be separated, the family decides to run away. They are almost caught by a band of greedy slave hunters, but the father makes a stirring "Declaration of Independence," vowing to fight to the death to remain a free man. Eventually they reach freedom in Canada.

The patient Uncle Tom is also separated from his family, but he never complains or loses his faith in God. Tom is a true Christian, showing

In this illustration of a dramatic scene from Uncle Tom's Cabin, Tom rescues little Eva, a young white girl, from drowning.

love and forgiveness even to those who abuse him. But when he refuses to tell where two runaway slaves are hiding, his owner has him beaten to death. Just before he dies, Tom's previous owner arrives to buy him back, but he is too late.

Although many of Stowe's descriptions of black people seem *racist* by today's standards, hers was the first American novel in which whites could read of black heroes who had great strength, dignity, intelligence, and religious feeling. No story had so successfully tried to show whites how it would feel to be enslaved. The book created an international uproar.

"It is one of the greatest triumphs recorded in literary history, to say nothing of the high-er triumph of its moral effect," wrote Henry Wadsworth Longfellow, the popular American poet. The German poet Heinrich Heine called *Uncle Tom's Cabin* the greatest book since the Bible. French novelist George Sand wrote, "It is no longer permissible to those who can read not to have read it." At that time, the written word was the only way people who were not face to face could communicate, because radio and television had not yet been invented. It is hard to imagine the sensation Stowe's book caused. *Uncle Tom's Cabin* was eagerly read by literally millions of people. Stowe became one of the world's most admired women. "How she is shaking the world with her *Uncle Tom's Cabin!*" Longfellow wrote in his diary. "At one step she has reached the top of the staircase up which the rest of us climb on our knees year after year."

Toys and games based on the book were popular, as were plays loosely based on the story. Stowe had no involvement with any of these performances, nor did she receive any money from them. Most of the plays completely distorted the book, intentionally weakening the antislavery message. Where Stowe had described Tom as powerful and intelligent, onstage he became cowardly and stupid. Black characters were played insultingly by white actors in "blackface" make-up. They sang songs such as "Happy Are We,

Countless stage versions of Stowe's story were presented before the Civil War. Most sensationalized the novel's plot and belittled blacks.

Darkies So Gay," and "Uncle Breve Tells about the Good Times He Had on the Old Plantation." It is probably because of these plays, rather than Stowe's book, that the name "Uncle Tom" is sometimes used today to insult blacks who are considered too eager to please whites.

The popularity of these plays in the North proved Stowe's point that northerners could be just as racist as southerners. But in the South, where the whole plantation system was built on slave labor, Stowe became the object of outright hatred. She received angry letters every day, and one package opened by her husband even contained an ear cut from a slave's head. Virginia schoolchildren learned to chant:

> Go, go, go
> Harriet Beecher Stowe
> We don't want you here in Virginny
> Go, go, go.

Opposing versions of slavery appeared in books like *Aunt Phyllis's Cabin; or Southern Life as It Is*. Many southerners claimed that slaves were happy and that Stowe knew nothing about slavery because she did not live in the South.

Stowe responded to these charges with another book, *A Key to Uncle Tom's Cabin*, published in 1853. In it she provided evidence for her depiction of slavery. She had personally witnessed families being broken apart at slave auctions in Cincinnati and had woven other true events into the story. Many of the characters were based on people she had met or read about. She had even written to Frederick Douglass, requesting a description of plantation life "from one who has been an actual laborer on one." The *Key* sold 100,000 copies, but Stowe was disappointed because few of her southern critics read it.

Harriet Beecher Stowe's success as a writer, however, did end the Stowes' worries about money. Her first payment for *Uncle Tom's Cabin* in 1852 had been $10,300, an enormous sum at the time. That same year, Calvin Stowe got a job in Andover, Massachusetts, that paid twice what he had earned at Bowdoin.

In 1856, the dispute over slavery was growing increasingly violent. Here, South Carolina congressman Preston Brooks beats antislavery Senator Charles Sumner of Massachusetts with a cane on the floor of the Senate.

After finishing the *Key*, Stowe took her first trip to Europe, where she was greeted as a hero by crowds of thousands. She collected $20,000 for the American abolitionist movement and received a letter "from the women of Great Britain to the women of America" calling for the end of slavery. The letter was signed by more than half a million women and filled 26 volumes.

In 1854, she published a book about her trip, *Sunny Memories of Foreign Lands*, after which she started a second antislavery novel. The book was called *Dred: A Tale of the Great Dismal Swamp*. In the book, an escaped slave named Dred lives among other blacks hiding out in the Dismal Swamp of North Carolina. Dred tries to start a rebellion, but he is shot by white slave hunters and dies in the swamp.

Stowe began the book with a respectful tone toward southerners. But since the passage of the Fugitive Slave Act, which was ignored by many northerners, the dispute over slavery had grown increasingly heated. In May 1856, the fanatical abolitionist John Brown slaughtered five pro-slavery settlers in Kansas. That same month Preston Brooks, a congressman from North Carolina, beat antislavery Senator Charles Sumner with a cane on the floor of the U.S. Senate. Sumner was a personal friend of Stowe's, and the angry author turned the conclusion of her book into a sharp attack on slaveholders.

Critics agreed *Dred* was not nearly as good a book as *Uncle Tom's Cabin*, but it quickly became a best-seller. Stowe wrote to her husband, "One hundred thousand copies . . . sold in four weeks! After that who cares what critics say?" The triumphant author made a second trip to England, this time meeting with Queen Victoria and Prince Albert. "The Queen seemed really delighted to see my wife," Calvin Stowe wrote afterward.

The Stowes received terrible news, however, on their return to America in June 1857. Their eldest son, 19-year-old Henry, had drowned in a boating accident. Henry's death brought back the depression that Stowe had not suffered since her days in Cincinnati. "I dread everything I do," she wrote. Still mourning her son, she wrote another book, this time about the injustice of the Calvinist God. Published in 1859, *The Minister's Wooing* compares the Calvinist route to salvation to a ladder from which the Puritan God had "knocked out every rung . . . but the highest."

But the issue of slavery soon reclaimed her attention. On October 16, 1859, John Brown led a raid on the U.S. arsenal at Harpers Ferry, Virginia. Brown captured weapons with the intention of leading a slave revolt, but he was caught and executed. Despite his violent methods, Stowe called Brown a hero "who calmly gave up his life to a noble effort for human freedom."

The prospects for a peaceful end to the dispute over slavery quickly faded. After Abraham Lincoln was elected president in 1860, 11 southern states *seceded*, or withdrew, from the United States and decided to form their own country, the Confederate States of America. The remaining states in the Union refused to allow the Confederates to secede. In 1861, Confederate troops attacked Fort Sumter in South Carolina, beginning the Civil War.

Stowe was glad that the North had finally taken up arms against the slaveholding South. She was not satisfied with President Lincoln's position on slavery, however, and wrote articles critical of him. President Lincoln's stated goal in fighting the war was to keep the country from breaking apart, not to end slavery.

Lincoln had taken political stands against slavery as early as 1837. He said he was "naturally anti-slavery" and could not remember when he "did not so think, and feel." He also believed, however, that the Constitution of the United States did not allow outsiders to end slavery in the states where it existed. Furthermore, he had to be careful not to offend the three slaveholding states that remained in the Union. Finally, though, after a victory at the Battle of Antietam strengthened his hand, Lincoln said he would issue an *Emancipa-*

In this scene from Uncle Tom's Cabin, *Eliza, a light-skinned black woman, escapes slavery in Kentucky by crossing the cracking ice of the Ohio river. Stowe based the episode on a true story.*

tion Proclamation that would free the slaves living in the enemy's territory.

In November 1862, Stowe paid a visit to the president to make sure he would follow through on his decision. Lincoln greeted her by saying, "So this is the little lady who made this great war." The two sat and talked for an hour, and Stowe was impressed with the president's kindness, decency, and honest intention to free the slaves. She never criticized him again.

On New Year's Day in 1863, Abraham Lincoln signed the Emancipation Proclamation. Although the warring southern states did not obey the decree, it clearly indicated that a Union victory would mean the end of slavery. In Massachusetts, a crowd filled the Boston Music Hall to celebrate the historic day. When Harriet Beecher Stowe was spotted in the audience, the hall was rocked with cheers of "Mrs. Stowe! Mrs. Stowe! Mrs. Stowe!" Stowe could only bow and wipe away her tears. The battle against slavery was nearing a victorious conclusion.

When Fred Stowe became an alcoholic, his mother tried desperately to find a cure until his disappearance in 1871.

5

Peace and Controversy

Change was coming rapidly not only to the nation but also to Harriet Beecher Stowe's family. Eighty-seven-year-old Lyman Beecher died in early 1863. "The old oak finally fell," Henry Ward Beecher wired his sister. Within a few years, Stowe began worshiping at an Episcopal church, completing her break with her father's religion.

That same year, Stowe's 21-year-old son Fred was wounded in the Battle of Gettysburg. Stowe had been proud that her son was one of the first to enlist in the Union army, but now she feared for his life. Her worries continued when he returned home in November. Already a heavy drinker before the war, he was now an alcoholic.

Stowe was comforted in this period by her husband, who in 1863 retired from Andover Seminary. Calvin Stowe was a gentle, loving man who never resented his wife's success. The couple decided to leave Andover, where they had lived for 12 years, and build a house in Hartford, Connecticut. The new house was a disaster. One night the pipes above Calvin Stowe's bed exploded. Drenched with water, he fell into the hallway sputtering, "Oh, yes, all the modern conveniences! Shower baths while you sleep!"

The house proved so expensive that Stowe was forced to write more than ever to pay the bills. She wrote everything from biographical sketches to short stories to travel pieces. Stowe was saddened by one of these articles: President Lincoln's obituary. The president had been shot by John Wilkes Booth on April 14, 1865, and had died the following morning.

That same month, the Civil War ended. Stowe mourned the terrible cost of the war—more than 600,000 people had been killed—but she was thrilled by the Union victory. The southern rebellion crushed, Congress passed the Thirteenth Amendment to the Constitution, ending slavery forever. In Stowe's 54th year, the day she had hoped, prayed, and worked so hard for had finally come.

But Stowe's joy was clouded by worries about her son Fred. Hoping to cure him of his drinking problem, she rented a thousand-acre cotton plantation in Florida for Fred to manage. On a visit in 1867, Stowe was delighted to find him tanned, happy, and sober. But a year later, Stowe returned to find the plantation in ruins and Fred in a drunken stupor. The failed project cost the Stowes $10,000.

Pressed for money, Stowe wrote 10 books between 1863 and 1870. She also wrote children's stories, religious poetry, and countless articles. One book, *Men of Our Times*, described 18 "lead-

The Union victory at the Battle of Gettysburg marked a turning point in the war, but Stowe's son Fred was one of many thousands wounded.

ing patriots of the day." They included Abraham Lincoln, Frederick Douglass, and her own brother Henry Ward Beecher, who was by now a nationally known minister. Another successful book was *Oldtown Folks*, which was based on the many funny stories Calvin Stowe had told her about his hometown in New England.

Still hoping her son Fred could redeem himself through hard work, Stowe bought a 200-acre orange grove in Mandarin, Florida. Fred ran the farm, and his parents lived there in the winter. Harriet spent her time sailing, picnicking, and raising money for the local church and school. Her husband spent most of the day sitting in his rocking chair on the front porch. On Sundays, he held services for both black and white worshipers. The Stowes' house became a tourist attraction, and postcards of their home were sold across the country.

Stowe had generally stayed away from controversy since the Civil War, but in 1869 and 1870 she once again risked her reputation to stand up for her beliefs. This time it was not the abuse of blacks that roused her anger but that of a woman.

During her 1856 visit to England, Stowe had become a close friend of mathematician Anne Isabella Milbanke Byron, the widow of Lord Byron. Lady and Lord Byron had been married only a year when she left him, returning to her parent's house with their infant daughter. It was commonly believed that Lady Byron had made the poet miserable and that it was she who had driven him to a life of excess and an early death. But Lady Byron confided to Stowe that it was Lord Byron who ruined their marriage. Byron had drunk too much, gambled, and, she said, had an affair with his own half sister.

Lady Byron never made public her grievances against her husband, and she died a few years after Stowe returned to America. But in 1868, Byron's last mistress published a memoir of the poet, blaming Lady Byron for his unhappiness. Harriet Beecher Stowe was especially angry at the attack because her friend was no longer alive to defend herself. Stowe decided to defend her friend's reputation by revealing Lady Byron's secret, including an account of Lord Byron's scandalous affair with his half sister. In the fall of 1869, the *Atlantic Monthly* published her article, "The True Story of Lady Byron's Life."

Stowe received much criticism for her account. The public was outraged at this woman who dared to criticize such an important man. The English government considered barring Stowe from the British Isles for defaming one of their national heroes. In America, readers were horrified by her story, and the *Atlantic* lost 15,000 subscribers.

Refusing to back down, Stowe expanded the article into a book, *Lady Byron Vindicated*, published in 1870. The response was again hostile. American poet Edmund Clarence Stedman called Lady Byron "a jealous virtuous prude" and Stowe "a gossiping green old granny." Stowe never regretted defending her friend, however, despite the criticism. Having fought so hard for the rights of blacks, she knew she could not ignore injustice against women. She told Horace Greeley, editor of the New York *Tribune*, "I consider Lady Byron's story as a type of the old idea of woman: that is, a creature to be crushed and trodden under foot whenever her fate and that of a man come in conflict." In 1871, as the storm over *Lady Byron Vindicated* gradually died down, Stowe turned 60. The Stowes now lived in a more modest house in Hartford. It was not as grand as their last house, but it was comfortable, and the backyard was big enough to play croquet. Next door lived another writer, Mark Twain. Increasingly, Stowe's life revolved around her family.

Her eldest daughters, the twins Eliza and Harriet, still lived at home and looked after their parents. Continuing the family tradition, the youngest daughter, Georgina, had married a minister, and the youngest Stowe, Charles, had become a preacher.

But Fred Stowe was heading for disaster. Unable to control his drinking, he gave in to despair. "I would kill myself and end it all," he told his mother one day, "but I know that you and all the family would feel the disgrace that such an end would bring upon you." In 1871, Fred Stowe sailed to California and was never heard from again. His mother was heartbroken. Not knowing if he was dead or alive, she never stopped hoping that he might return.

One final family crisis awaited her, this time involving her brother Henry Ward Beecher. By the early 1870s, he was the most admired and influential clergyman and reformer in the country. Beecher was an extremely popular speaker, known for his dramatic style. Mark Twain wrote that when Beecher spoke, he "went marching up and down the stage waving his arms in the air, hurling sarcasms this way and that, discharging rockets of poetry, and exploding mines of eloquence, halting now and then to stamp his foot three times in succession to emphasize a point."

But Henry Ward Beecher's fortunes began to change when he publicly insulted Victoria

The house where the Stowes spent their winters in Mandarin, Florida, became a tourist attraction; it even appeared on postcards.

Woodhull, an advocate of women's rights and "free love," the idea that sexual relations outside marriage were morally acceptable. Beecher called Woodhull a prostitute. She responded on November 2, 1872, with a special issue of her newspaper, the *Weekly*. In it she accused Beecher of carrying on a long-term love affair with Elizabeth Tilton, the wife of one of his friends. Tilton's husband,

67

Theodore, sued Beecher for adultery in 1874. Although the jury was unable to reach a verdict and Beecher was acquitted, the article and Tilton's lawsuit caused a sensational scandal that was splashed across the front pages of newspapers around the country.

Harriet Beecher Stowe refused to believe a word of the charges against her brother or to listen to any of the evidence.

In 1871, she published a series of magazine articles in the form of a novel entitled *My Wife and I*. The book contained a character based on Victoria Woodhull named Audacia Dangereyes who is dangerously radical and immoral. Other strong-willed women are shown positively, however, reflecting Stowe's more quiet feminism.

Stowe also launched a new career during this period. Athough she had never made a speech before in her life, at the age of 61 she went on the road to give lectures. Her first speaking appearance was a flop. She was so nervous that her voice wavered and cracked. Some members of the audience walked out before she finished.

But Stowe came from a family of orators, and she refused to give up. Before one important reading, she playfully brushed her white hair up to the top of her head and called a friend to come see. "Now, my dear, gaze upon me," she said. "I am exactly like my father when he was going to preach." This time her performance was a success.

Soon her readings of *Uncle Tom's Cabin* drew great praise. One Pittsburgh critic reported, "Her voice is low, just tinged with huskiness, but is quite musical." As a friend of Stowe's pointed out, listeners "could not fail to understand what her words had signified to the generation that had passed through the struggle of our war."

When Stowe turned 70, the *Atlantic Monthly*, which had published many of her stories over the years, honored her with a grand birthday party. Some of New England's most prominent writers wrote tributes to Stowe, and Henry Ward

Beecher gave an emotional speech. Although she was delighted by the show of love and admiration, Stowe did not forget her original goals. Solemnly addressing the assembled guests, she spoke of the progress southern blacks had made since the end of slavery and of the work that still had to be done to right past injustices.

Both Harriet Beecher Stowe and her husband were by now in bad health, and travel became increasingly difficult for them. They gave up their Florida winters and settled year-round in Hartford. Calvin Stowe became seriously ill, and Harriet told a friend, "He requires personal attentions that only a wife ought to render." But she welcomed their time together, saying in 1884, "I think we have never enjoyed each other's society more than this winter." In 1886, after a long illness, Calvin Stowe died in his wife's arms.

Stowe was devastated by her loss, but she continued to pursue life energetically. In 1886, Scottish evangelist Henry Drummond described her as a "wonderfully agile old lady, as fresh as a squirrel still, but with the face and air of a lion. I have not been so taken with any one on this side of the Atlantic."

Time took its toll, however, and Stowe suffered a mild stroke from which she never completely recovered. She became increasingly eccentric and confused. Finally, she died of natural causes on July 1, 1896. She was 85 years old.

When Stowe was buried in the family plot in Andover, Massachusetts, her friends and relatives gathered by her grave and sang a hymn that Stowe herself had composed. It reflects both her faith in God and her acceptance of death:

Stowe called her bald, bearded, and portly husband "my little rabbi," a nickname that delighted the biblical scholar.

It lies around us like a cloud,
A world we do not see
Yet the sweet closing of an eye
May bring us there to be.

After Stowe's death, millions around the world mourned the passing of a woman whose faith, integrity, and idealism had made her one of the most celebrated writers of the 19th century. As poet Elizabeth Barrett Browning remarked of Stowe, "She above all women (yes, and men of the age) has moved the world—and *for good*."

In her 33 books and countless articles, Stowe promoted simple virtues, celebrated the worth of all people—black and white, male and female—and above all, attacked racial injustice. *Uncle Tom's Cabin*, according to American author Henry James, was "for an immense number of people, much less a book than a state of vision." Stowe's vision of freedom and equality lives on today.

Further Reading

Other Biographies of Harriet Beecher Stowe

Ash, Maureen. *The Story of Harriet Beecher Stowe.*
Chicago: Children's Press, 1990.

Rouverol, Jean. *Harriet Beecher Stowe: Woman
Crusader.* New York: Putnam, 1968.

Scott, John Anthony. *Woman Against Slavery: The Story
of Harriet Beecher Stowe.* New York: Crowell, 1978.

Related Books

Birdoff, Harry. *The World's Greatest Hit: Uncle Tom's
Cabin.* New York: S. F. Vanni, 1947.

Johnston, Johanna. *Harriet and the Runaway Book.* New
York: Harper & Row, 1977.

Chronology

June 14, 1811   Harriet Elizabeth Beecher is born in Litchfield, Connecticut.

1816   Roxana Foote Beecher, Harriet's mother, dies of tuberculosis.

1832   Beecher family moves to Cincinnati, Ohio.

1833   Harriet Elizabeth Beecher's first newspaper article is published

1836   Beecher marries Calvin Stowe.

1850   Calvin and Harriet Beecher Stowe move to Brunswick, Maine.

1852   *Uncle Tom's Cabin* is published.

1853   Stowes travel to Europe.

1856   *Dred: A Tale of the Great Dismal Swamp* is published.

1860   Abraham Lincoln is elected president; seven southern states secede from the

Union and form the Confederate States of America.

1861 Confederate troops attack Fort Sumter, marking the start of the Civil War.

1862 Stowe meets with President Lincoln.

1863 President Lincoln signs the Emancipation Proclamation; the Stowes move to Hartford, Connecticut.

1865 John Wilkes Booth assassinates President Lincoln; the Civil War ends; Congress enacts the Thirteenth Amendment to the Constitution, outlawing slavery.

1869 *Oldtown Folks* is published; Stowe buys Mandarin, Florida, estate.

1870 *Lady Byron Vindicated* is published.

1878 Stowe's last novel, *Poganuc People*, is published.

1886 Calvin Stowe dies in Hartford.

July 1, 1896 Harriet Beecher Stowe dies at the age of 85.

Glossary

abolitionist   a person who supported the movement to abolish, or end, slavery and the slave trade in the United States

academy   a private secondary school

amendment   a change in the U.S. Constitution requiring formal approval by three-fourths of the states

cholera   an infectious, often fatal disease, marked by vomiting and stomach cramps

Civil War   the conflict between northern states (the Union) and rebelling southern states (the Confederacy) during the years 1861–65

clergyman   a minister, priest, or rabbi who is authorized to conduct religious services

Congress   lawmaking body of the U.S. federal government, consisting of the Senate and the House of Representatives

orator   a person skilled in the art of public speaking

Puritanism   a religious reform movement in England and New England during the 16th and 17th centuries that opposed the ceremonial worship of the Church of England

Quakers   members of the Society of Friends, a religious group whose members believe that no priest or ritual is needed to communicate with God; Quakers believe in the equality of men and women of all races, and they oppose war

racist   prejudiced on the basis of race or employing racial stereotypes

secede   to withdraw from membership in an organization or union

slaughterhouse   a building in which animals are butchered for food

spa   a resort that has mineral springs

tuberculosis   a contagious disease caused by a very small organism that affects the lungs

Underground Railroad   a network of people all over the United States who helped runaway slaves escape to free states and Canada

Index

Abolitionist movement, 11, 12, 50

Albert, Prince, 52

Andover, Massachusetts, 49, 71

Andover Seminary, 58

Antietam, Battle of, 54

Beecher, Catharine, 11, 24, 25, 27, 29, 31, 36

Beecher, Harriet Porter (stepmother), 19–21

Beecher, Henry Ward, 14, 25, 36, 57, 62, 66–68, 69

Beecher, Isabella (sister-in-law), 12

Beecher, Lyman (father), 17–19, 22, 24, 25–27, 57

Beecher, Roxana (mother), 17

Booth, John Wilkes, 58

Bowdoin College, 39, 49

Brooks, Preston, 51

Brown, John, 51, 52–53

Brunswick, Maine, 8

Byron, Isabella Millbanke, 63–64, 65

Byron, Lord, 24, 63, 64

Cholera, 11

Cincinatti, Ohio, 8, 11, 12, 27, 29, 31, 36, 39, 49, 52

Civil War, 53, 59, 62

Confederate States of America, 53

Constitution, U.S., 54, 59

Douglass, Frederick, 42, 49, 62

Dutton, Mary, 30, 37

Emancipation Proclamation, 54–55

Fort Sumter, 53

Fugitive Slave Act, 12, 41, 51

Gettysburg, Battle of, 57

Harpers Ferry, Virginia, 52

Hartford, Connecticut, 24, 58, 70

Lady Byron Vindicated, 64, 65,

Lane Seminary, 27, 31–32, 37

Lincoln, Abraham, 15, 53–54, 55, 58, 59–62

National Era, 11, 15

New York *Tribune,* 65

"Porkopolis," 29. *See also* Cincinnati

Quakers. See Society of Friends

Slavery, 7, 8, 12, 14, 30, 41, 42, 43, 49
Society of Friends, 42
Stowe, Calvin (husband), 8, 31, 36, 37, 38, 52, 62, 70
Stowe, Charles (son), 65
Stowe, Eliza (daughter), 33, 65
Stowe, Frederick (son), 37, 57, 65–66
Stowe, Georgiana May (daughter), 37
Stowe, Harriet (daughter), 33, 65
Stowe, Harriet Beecher
    and abolition, 11–12, 14, 55
    as speaker, 68–69
    childhood, 17, 21–22
    death, 71
    in Europe, 50, 63
    in Florida, 62
    married life, 32, 33, 36, 37, 39
    teaching career, 25, 31
    writing career, 11–12, 14, 33, 37, 49, 50, 52, 59, 62, 64, 68
Stowe, Henry (son), 36, 52
Stowe, Samuel (son), 39
Sumner, Charles, 51

Thirteenth Amendment, 59
Tilton, Elizabeth, 67–68
Turner, Nat, 42
Twain, Mark, 65, 66

Uncle Tom's Cabin, 8, 14, 31, 39, 41, 43–48, 51, 69, 72
    sales of, 14, 15
    toys and games, 46
Underground Railroad, 36, 42

Victoria, Queen, 52

Western Female Institute, 31
Woodhull, Victoria, 67

Celia Bland is a poet and freelance writer living in Brooklyn, New York. She has taught creative writing at New York University and literature at Parsons School of Design, published poetry in numerous literary journals, and participated in poetry readings in the United States and abroad.

Picture Credits